W9-CEB-242

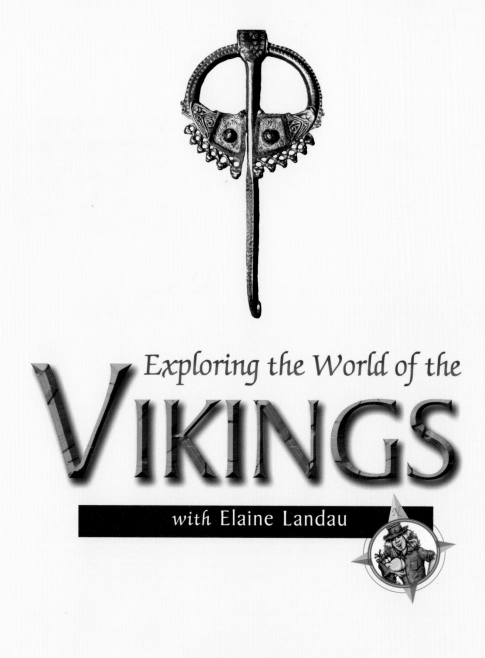

Exploring the World of the

VIKINGS

with Elaine Landau

Enslow Elementary

an imprint of

Enslow Publishers, Inc.

40 Industrial Road	PO Box 38
Box 398	Aldershot
Berkeley Heights, NJ 07922	Hants GU12 6BP
USA	UK

http://www.enslow.com

"The 'Exploring Ancient Civilizations With Elaine Landau' series tells the stories of the Egyptians, Greeks, Romans, Chinese, Vikings, and Aztecs with texts and illustrations designed to appeal to a broad spectrum of students. While not refraining from acknowledging injustice, hardship, and even the brutality of pre-modern civilizations, the series nonetheless succeeds in presenting these six ancient peoples in a dignified, praiseworthy, and even exemplary light. Highly recommended."
—Nicholas F. Jones, Professor of Classics, University of Pittsburgh

Enslow Elementary, an imprint of Enslow Publishers, Inc.

Enslow Elementary ® is a registered trademark of Enslow Publishers, Inc.

Library of Congress Cataloging-in-Publication Data

Landau, Elaine.
    Exploring the world of the Vikings with Elaine Landau / Elaine Landau.— 1st ed.
       p. cm. — (Exploring ancient civilizations with Elaine Landau)
    Includes bibliographical references and index.
    ISBN 0-7660-2340-0
    1. Vikings—Juvenile literature. 2. Civilization, Viking—Juvenile literature. I. Title. II. Series.
    CL65.L36 2005
    948'.022--dc22

                      2004016152

Printed in the United States of America

10 9 8 7 6 5 4 3 2 1

To Our Readers: We have done our best to make sure all Internet addresses in this book were active and appropriate when we went to press. However, the author and the publisher have no control over and assume no liability for the material available on those Internet sites or on other Web sites they may link to. Any comments or suggestions can be sent by e-mail to comments@enslow.com or to the address on the back cover.

Illustration Credits:
All illustrations of Elaine and Max by David Pavelonis.

© Artville, L.L.C. All rights reserved., p. 8; **©2004 Werner Forman / TopFoto / The Image Works, p. 16**; ©AAAC / Topham / The Image Works, pp. 1, 20 (bottom), 32 (bottom), 40 (top), 45 (top); Courtesy of U.S. Naval Academy Museum, painting by Edward Moran, p. 26; ©CM Dixon / HIP / The Image Works, pp. 2, 12, 31; ©Enslow Publishers, Inc., pp. 4–5; Clipart.com. , pp. 4, 6 (bottom), 10 (top), 12 (inset), 15, 17, 19, 29, 30 (top), 34 (main), 39 (top), 40 (bottom), 46, 47; ©Museum of London / HIP / The Image Works, p. 11; Library of Congress, pp. 14 (bottom), 15, 21, 37 (top); ©Ted Spiegel / The Image Works, pp. 30 (bottom,), 33; ©ARPL / HIP / The Image Works , p. 39 (bottom); ©Ancient Art & Architecture Collection Ltd ©AAAC / Topham / The Image Works, pp. 24, 45 (middle);©AAAC / Topham / The Image Works pp. 20, 45 (top); ©ARPL / HIP / The Image Works, pp. 24 (top); Werner Forman Archive/ Viking Ship Museum, Bygdoy . Location: 04. ©2004 Werner Forman / TopFoto / The Image Works, p. 23 (top); ©Copyright: Ancient Art & Architecture Collection Ltd ©AAAC / Topham / The Image Works, p. 24 (bottom); Werner Forman Archive/ Viking Ship Museum, Bygdoy . Location: 03. ©2004 Werner Forman / TopFoto / The Image Works, p. 25; Painet, Inc., pp. 34 (inset), 35 (top); ©Topham / The Image Works , 23 (bottom), 28; Associated Press, AP: Photographer John Rasmussen, p. 41; National Aeronautics and Space Administration, p. 42 (top); Corel Corporation, pp. 7 (top), 9, 13, 19, 22, 27, 32, 36, 37, (bottom), 38 (top), 45 (bottom); Elaine Landau, p. 43.

Front Cover Illustrations: David Pavelonis (Elaine & Max drawings); Viking longships under sail, 20th century. "Drakkar", watercolor by Albert Sebille. ©ARPL / HIP / The Image Works (main image); Gotland, Sweden: Marteus Box Brooch, gold and silver 1000 AD. VIKING. ©AAAC / Topham / The Image Works (top, right); Corel Corporation (bottom, right)

Back Cover Illustrations: David Pavelonis (Elaine & Max drawing); Figurehead of a Viking ship. 8th century. Viking artifact, Ancient Art & Architecture Collection Ltd ©AAAC / Topham / The Image Works (left).

Contents

		The World of the Vikings	4
		Dear Fellow Explorer	6
Chapter	1	Out Into the World— Viking Explorers	8
Chapter	2	Raiders—Attack at Dawn	11
Chapter	3	Viking Society	15
Chapter	4	The World of Work	19
Chapter	5	Viking Ships	22
Chapter	6	Viking Traders	25
Chapter	7	Religion	28
Chapter	8	Housing	33
Chapter	9	Food	36
Chapter	10	Clothing	39
Chapter	11	Heading Home	41
		Farewell Fellow Explorer	43
		Timeline	44
		Glossary	45
		For More Information	46
		Internet Addresses	47
		Index	48

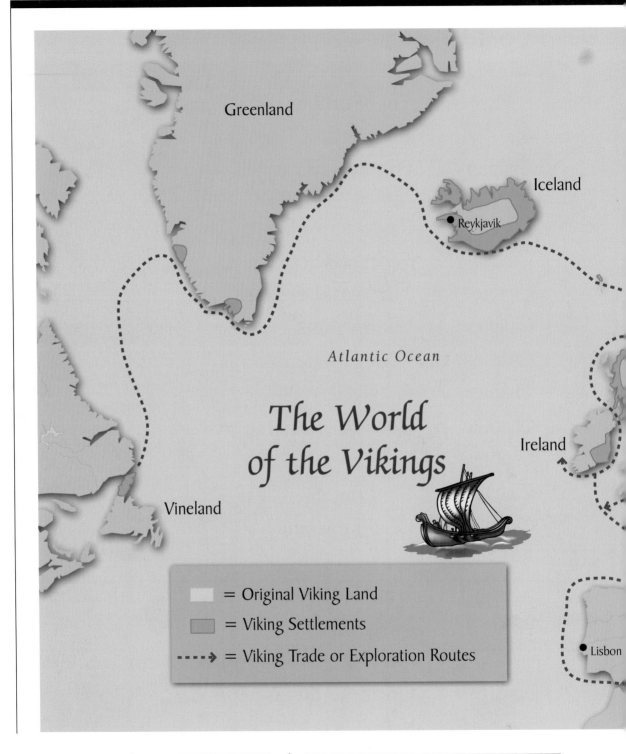

Greenland

Iceland

● Reykjavik

Atlantic Ocean

The World
of the Vikings

Ireland

Vineland

● Lisbon

    = Original Viking Land

    = Viking Settlements

----→ = Viking Trade or Exploration Routes

Norwegion
Sea

Scandinavia

Oslo

Baltic
Sea

Britain

Constantinople

Bysantium

Africa

Dear Fellow Explorer,

What if you could travel back in time? If you could go anywhere in the world, where would you stop? Would visiting an ancient civilization interest you? If you like adventure and sea travel, pick a time from the late 700s to 1100. Then head straight for northern Europe.

At that time and place, there lived a bold and daring group of people. They were called Norsemen or Northmen. Later they became known as Vikings.

Some felt the name fit them well. In the Old Norse language, to go "a-viking" means to go pirating. The Vikings were famous pirates and raiders. People feared their ruthless attacks.

Yet the Vikings were much more than just fierce fighters. They were also fearless, intrepid explorers and successful traders. They

Viking ships crossed the sea in search of new lands.

The green fields and mountains of Iceland were the sites for Viking villages. This is Stokknes, Iceland.

traveled to distant lands to start towns. Vikings were farmers, shipbuilders, and outstanding craftsmen as well.

I'm Elaine Landau and this is my loyal dog Max. Max and I are about to take a trip back in time to the Viking Age. The trip was Max's idea. He has always wanted to sail on a Viking ship. Join us in the pages ahead. There's a lot to see. Don't worry about the time—with time travel, you can always be back before dinner!

Out Into the World—Viking Explorers

*T*he Vikings never lived in just one nation. They never had a single ruler either. Instead, by the year 800, there were three major Viking kingdoms. These were in an area now known as Scandinavia. It includes the present-day nations of Sweden, Denmark, and Norway.

These different Viking groups had much in common. They spoke a language called Old Norse. They worshiped similar gods. They also had similar customs or ways of doing things.

During the seventh century, many Viking families had farms. They grew crops and raised farm animals. However, parts of Scandinavia did not have a lot of farmland. In some places, the soil was poor. This was especially true in the mountains of Norway.

Over time, there were more

Scandinavia is made up of the present-day nations of Sweden, Denmark, and Norway.

The final stop in Vikings' expansion across the Atlantic Ocean was North America. The name Vineland probably came from the Old Norse word "vin," meaning field or meadow.

and more Vikings. Land was needed to raise crops and support their growing numbers. Viking men went to sea to search for new areas. They picked places where they could farm and where their animals had enough to eat. They hoped to start homes there.

By about 870, Vikings settled in Iceland as well as began building homes in England. In 911, other Vikings settled in the Normandy area of France. Then, in 982, Vikings began building new towns in Greenland. Thousands of Viking families went to live there.

The Vikings even came to North America. They were there long before Christopher Columbus in 1492. In about 1000, Viking Leif Eriksson had arrived on the Atlantic coast. He started a settlement called Vineland in Newfoundland, Canada. The Vikings did not stay at

The Vikings sailed to Iceland, Greenland, and parts of North America.

Vineland very long. They had problems with the people there. Yet the Vikings left proof that their colony existed. In 1962, researchers at the Newfoundland site found the remains of many Viking houses. They also found some tools, jewelry, and carvings.

Some people believe that Viking explorers may have also traveled to the area now known as the United States. A Viking coin was recently uncovered in Maine. However, there is nothing else that proves there was a colony there.

Raiders—Attack at Dawn

*T*he Vikings sailed near and far. They did not always come in peace. Vikings were fierce raiders and fighters. Groups of them would suddenly arrive by ship. It was a terrifying sight.

The Vikings especially liked to loot churches and monasteries. Monasteries were places where monks lived and worked. A monk was a type of church leader. Often valuable religious items were kept there. The first recorded Viking raid occurred in 793. It took place at a monastery on an island off England's coast.

The Vikings also attacked villages and centers where people traded goods. These raiders took anything of

Vikings raided villages to get treasure. In reality, there is no proof that Vikings had horns on their helmets.

When Vikings raided a village they sometimes lit arrows and shot them into the roofs of homes. The homes would then light on fire.

value. During their raids, the Vikings killed men, women, and children. In those days, attacks were often quite brutal. The Vikings were not very different from other raiders from other civilizations of the time.

At times, Vikings took people and made them slaves. Some were made to work on farms. Others were sold by Viking traders.

These chessmen represent Viking warriors. The figures were carved from walrus ivory in the 12th century.

Whatever his normal job, a Viking man often had to go on raids. A helmet protected the head and face during battle.

Vikings usually struck as the sun was rising. They wanted to surprise their victims. They would often leave as quickly as they arrived. However, in some cases, the Vikings did not leave. They stayed and took over the village.

By the early 800s, the Vikings had gone on numerous raids. At first, these mostly took place in England, Scotland, and Ireland. Later they raided parts of Belgium and the Netherlands. The Vikings continued to attack and loot. During the mid-800s, different Viking groups attacked different places. They struck areas in France, Spain, and Italy.

But by about 1100, these raids were largely over. The various nations in Europe had grown stronger. They built powerful armies and navies. Now well-trained fighting men met the Vikings' surprise advances.

Sometimes the Vikings remained in the areas they attacked. They would build new Viking settlements. When other Vikings attacked years later, they fought hard to defend their homes and settlements as well. These well-prepared forces began to defeat the Viking raiders.

There was still another reason why the raids stopped. The Vikings became Christians. The Norse religion had glorified battle. Since the Vikings no longer followed it, many of them wanted to change their ways. After three hundred years of raiding, the period known as the Viking Age finally ended around the year 1100.

A Viking warrior fought with a broad two-edged blade made of iron or steel.

Viking Society

*V*iking society was made up of classes. At the top were the Viking kings or chiefs. They made laws and gave out punishments.

These kings were quite rich. All owned large amounts of land. Often Viking kings were the sons and grandsons of kings. However, the right to rule was not theirs by birth. An unjust or cruel king could lose his position.

There were some differences among the various Viking groups. While Viking kingdoms had kings, the smaller Viking settlements in Iceland did not. These smaller settlements had assemblies called Things. The Things were made up of free farmers who owned land. They helped settle disputes. They also decided how wrongdoers would be punished.

Erik the Red was a Viking chief and the father of Leif Eriksson. Erik the Red was a leader of a Viking settlement in Greenland. When Erik the Red died, his son, Leif, became leader.

Every summer the chiefs of all the Things in Iceland came together in a nationwide assembly. This assembly was called the Althing. It met for one or two weeks. At this meeting, larger problems were dealt with. Often, important decisions were made about going to war.

Rank mattered in Viking society. Beneath the king were the nobles. Like the king, these men were rich

The Iceland Althing met annually from the year 930 at Thingvellir or Parliament Plains. The open-air site is set before a natural wall of lava.

The inside of a Viking home might have look like this one. The men are working on swords while the woman finishes a household chore.

landowners. Under the nobles were the free men. These were the merchants, craftsmen, and farmers.

Slaves were on the lowest level. At times these people had been taken during raids. Certain crimes were also punished by slavery. Though slaves belonged to their owners, they had some protection under Viking law. Slaves could earn their freedom through work. At that point, they were usually given some land and farm animals for their own use.

Family life was important in Viking society. The husband was the head of the household. Yet women had certain rights. Viking wives could own property. They were also permitted to divorce their husbands.

Viking women were expected to care for their homes

and their children. However, sometimes they had to do much more. When their husbands were away on raids, they took charge. Many ran large farms.

Family ties were very strong. The family included grandparents, aunts, uncles, and cousins. Family members were fiercely loyal to one another. At times, disputes broke out between different families. In some cases, this led to ongoing fights and arguments that could last for years.

Viking children did not go to school. They learned from their parents and other adults. Young girls were taught to cook, make cloth, and sew. Most boys learned to hunt, fish, farm, and fight. Both boys and girls would help with the farm work.

*T*he Vikings were well known for their raids. For this reason, many people think that was all they did. This is not true. There was much more to Viking life.

Most Vikings were farmers. They grew a number of crops. These included fruits, vegetables, barley, rye, and oats. Often farmers kept farm animals, too.

Vikings were also hunters. They hunted deer, elk, bears, wild boars, and other animals. Bands of men hunted whales together. During the

Besides farm animals, the Vikings relied on hunting for food. Sometimes they would hunt for elk.

Vikings used many different tools. This axe head could have been used to chop wood for a fire or for building houses.

cold winter months in the northern lands, they hunted seals and walruses as well. Fishermen caught herring, cod, and other fish. Craftsmen were kept very busy. This was especially true for metalsmiths. They used iron and other metals to make weapons. Viking warriors needed helmets, swords, shields, armor, hatchets, and clubs.

Other craftsmen made beautiful gold, silver, and bronze jewelry. They designed necklaces, bracelets, rings, brooches, and pendants. Carpenters made stools, chests, benches, and ships. Craftsmen working with leather made pouches, shoes, and boots.

This Viking box brooch is made of silver and gold. It was made about 1000 A.D.

This is how you spell the word "Viking" in runes.

The Vikings had their own system of writing. They used symbols called runes. Like the letters in our alphabet, the different runes represented sounds. Each rune also had its own special meaning. Using these symbols, the Vikings left quite a few documents carved in stone, wood, and metal.

At times, runes were used for more than writing. These symbols were also believed to have supernatural or magical powers. They were sometimes used to try to cast spells and tell fortunes. Experts called rune masters were asked to do this. These individuals were highly respected for their skill. As a Viking saying goes: "Let no man carve runes to cast a spell, save first he learns to read them well."

Ancient Viking symbols called runes were often carved into stone.

Viking Ships

*T*he sea was an important part of Viking life. Scandinavia is mostly surrounded by water. Norway also has many fjords. These are inlets that lead out to the sea. Often Vikings traveled from Norway to Sweden by boat. This was easier than crossing the mountains. That may be why the Vikings became outstanding shipbuilders.

Most Viking ships could be either sailed or rowed. They were made to ride on stormy ocean waters. Yet they could also glide down a shallow river.

The fjords of Norway were the bases for the early Viking raiders.

Sometimes the Vikings carved dragon heads onto the fronts of their boats.

The Vikings built different vessels for different purposes. These included ships for trading and ones for raiding. Those used by traders were known as knarrs. A trader's ship was broader than the ones used for war. It had to carry cargo (goods) back and forth. Most of these ships were about fifty to sixty-five feet long.

Viking warships were long, slender, and fast moving. They were called drakkars. Many of these vessels were fifty-five to

YOU OUGHT TO SEE THE VIEW FROM UP HERE.

This replica of a Viking ship sails through the icy waters of Greenland.

A drakkar was a special type of Viking ship.

seventy-five feet long. Sometimes at the prow was a dragon's head carved out of wood. These ships looked like huge sea monsters.

Warships usually carried at least fifty men. Some ships could also sail with horses. These were designed to go right up to the coastline. The men would mount their horses and attack.

This figurehead is from an eighth century Viking ship.

Viking Traders

he Vikings were outstanding seamen and traders. They easily traveled to faraway ports. The Vikings had many things to trade. Areas of Scandinavia were filled with forests. Logs from these forests could be used to build ships and houses. People in other parts of the world wanted the logs, which were also called timber. Timber became a highly valued trade item.

Iron and amber were found in Scandinavia as well. Iron was used to make tools and weapons. Amber beads were used in jewelry. These were in demand too.

The Vikings also traded many other items. People in warmer regions wanted walrus skins. These were used to make ship ropes. Whale bones were desired

This Viking ship is in a museum in Oslo, Norway.

The Vikings were far-reaching explorers and traders, traveling from their Scandinavian homeland to the New World in the west and to Baghdad and beyond in the east.

as well. They made wonderful carving tools. The Vikings also traded fur pelts.

In Scandinavia, people eagerly awaited the traders' return. They brought home wonderful items. Among these were gold, weapons, and wine. They also brought back salt, pottery, glass, spices, and silk.

Sometimes Viking traders used silver coins to pay for things. More often, however, they bartered for goods. This means that they traded something they had for something they wanted.

The Vikings opened up exciting new trade routes. They traveled thousands of miles to get to markets. Some were as far away as present-day Baghdad in Iraq.

Vikings used animal fur to keep themselves warm during the harsh, cold winters.

Religion

The Vikings had many gods and goddesses. They prayed to different gods for different reasons. Their most important one was Odin. He was the god of battle and wisdom. Other gods called him the All-Father. He was their leader preparing for the final battle against evil.

Odin had only one eye. He traded his other eye for a drink from the Well of Wisdom. This water made him even wiser. Odin rode an eight-legged horse named Sleipnir. He also had two pet ravens. Their names were Hugin, meaning Thought, and Munin, meaning Memory.

During the day, Odin let the birds fly throughout the world. They would return to him each night. Then they would sit on Odin's shoulders and tell him all they had seen and heard. Odin was also

Odin was the head of all the Viking gods.

known as Woden. The word "Wednesday" comes from his name, and was once called "Woden's Day."

Thor was one of Odin's sons. He was the god of thunder and lightning. Thor was "the protector of society." He was an extremely popular Viking god. Thor's Day became the word "Thursday."

Frey was the god of harvest and fruitfulness. He made sure that there was sunshine and rain for the crops to grow well. The word "Friday" comes from his name, and was called "Frey's day." Frey's twin sister was the goddess Freya. Freya was the goddess of love, beauty, and fruitfulness. She had lovely golden hair. Freya guided women who died in childbirth to the next world.

Loki was the jester or prankster who lived among the gods. However, he was not actually a god. He was the son of giants, who were sworn enemies of the gods. He was quick-witted and extremely clever. Sometimes he played harmless jokes and tricks on others to make the gods laugh. At other

Thor drove a chariot, which caused thunder, and created lightning with his hammer.

Valhalla, meaning "Hall of the Slain," was where Odin met and ate with dead Viking heroes.

times his mischievous nature could be dangerous. He was known to create evil plots as well. Loki could never be trusted.

At special times of the year, the Vikings held religious ceremonies. Many were outdoors. Usually an animal would be killed. This was done in honor of a god or goddess. Then, there would be great feasting and celebrating.

The Vikings did not believe that life ended at death. They thought that there was a life after death in Valhalla, the Viking heaven. Vikings were buried with food, furniture, weapons, jewelry, and other things. These

This face was carved on a cart that was found buried with a Viking and his ship.

items showed how wealthy and important that person was in life.

Kings and other important people were buried in their ships. These vessels were to carry them into the next world. Sometimes funeral ships were buried under mounds of earth. These looked like small hills. Other times the ships were burned in piles called funeral pyres. Many Vikings were not buried in real ships. Instead, they had stones placed around their graves in the shape of a ship.

IT LOOKS LIKE THAT KING LIVED WELL.

Vikings often put stones around a grave. These stone were often placed in the shape of an oval, triangle, or a ship.

By the end of the tenth century, the Vikings no longer believed in their gods. Christians had come to Scandinavia to spread their beliefs. They convinced the Viking kings of Denmark, Sweden, and Norway to become Christians. Once their leaders were Christian, the people accepted this new faith as well.

Some Vikings became Christians. This silver cross was made in the eleventh century and was found in Norway.

*E*arly Viking houses were called longhouses. They were basically just one long room. Different materials were used to build these. It depended on what people found where they lived. Some houses were made of stone or wood. Other places, the walls were made of squares of sod or grassy soil.

Most Viking homes had thatched roofs made of straw or reeds. Reeds were thick stalks from certain plants.

Danish scouts learn how the Vikings lived by reconstructing a Viking town.

The roofs were held up by two rows of posts. These rows were placed down the center of the room.

Also in the room's center was a long hearth, or fireplace. The Vikings depended on the hearth for warmth during the cold months and light during the nighttime. They also used it to cook their food. There was a hole in the roof above the fire. This was to let the smoke out. However, the room was usually still somewhat smoky.

These people sit in a recreation of a Viking house (above). A house would have a hole in the roof so the smoke from the fire could escape (left).

The Viking settlement at L'Anse aux Meadows on the coast of Newfoundland has been reconstructed as it might have looked around the year 1000.

The family sat in front of fire when they ate. They also slept near the fire. It was important to keep warm during the night.

Yet Viking homes could still be chilly. There was a reason for this. Small open spaces for windows were cut into the walls. However, these windows did not have glass panes. Instead, shutters made of wood could be pulled over them. The wood shutters helped, but they never kept out all the cold night air.

Food

*T*he Vikings were tied to the sea in many ways. Much of their food came from it. Vikings living on the coast ate lots of fish. Cod, herring, and haddock were favorites. Vikings living farther inland enjoyed freshwater fish. They caught trout, eels, and other fish from rivers and lakes.

Vikings were meat eaters too. They raised farm animals for food. These included sheep, cattle, pigs, and geese. They also ate deer, elk, wild boars, hares, and ducks. In

Vikings on the coast often ate animals that they caught in the sea, such as whales.

more northern regions, Vikings ate reindeer, seals, and whales too.

This Viking helmet is decorated with a picture of a deer.

Fruits and berries were also part of their diet. The women gathered these from wooded areas. Farmers grew fruit trees. Cabbage, onions, and peas were grown on farms as well.

Vikings usually washed down their meals with beer. Many also liked mead. This was an alcoholic beverage. It was made from honey, spices, water, and other ingredients. Wealthy Vikings sometimes drank imported

The Vikings raised sheep for meat and wool.

Viking women would gather berries from wooded areas.

wine. They bought it from traders who had gone to other countries.

Viking women cooked for much of the day. For breakfast they usually prepared porridges made from barley and oats. The main meal was served in the evening. It was a welcome treat after a hard day's work.

Winters in Viking country could be harsh. The Vikings needed warm clothing. Viking women spun wool on large looms. They made woolen pants and long woolen tunics for the men. Often the tunics had fancy borders. Those made for wealthy men were sometimes embroidered with gold and silver threads.

This Viking man wears a tunic with a woolen cloak.

Outdoors, the men wore woolen cloaks. Their cloaks were fastened at the shoulder with a brooch. This left their arms free to reach for their swords. Sometimes the cloaks were edged with imported silk or fancy braiding.

Viking men often wore leather caps or fur hats. They also had woolen or fur gloves. Fur-lined boots helped keep their feet warm during the winter.

This sculpture of a Viking man shows him wearing a pointed helmet.

This pin is made of silver and was worn once by some lucky Viking.

Viking women wore long dresses. Over that they had a shorter garment that looked something like an apron. Rich Viking women fastened it at the shoulder straps with two large brooches. Married women wore white linen headdresses. For a Viking woman, this headdress was a badge of honor. It showed her position as the married mistress of the household.

Vikings enjoyed wearing jewelry. Both men and women wore bracelets on their arms and wrists. Many had necklaces and rings as well. They were also fond of large beautiful brooches. These had two uses. They were lovely to look at. Yet they were also used to fasten clothing.

These women are dressed in traditional Viking clothing.

Heading Home

Max and I enjoyed learning about the Vikings. Though they lived long ago, we are still reminded of them today. Quite a few English words come from Viking words. These include "knife," "skull," "window," "husband," "sky," and "ill."

Many villages and towns in the United States and Canada have Viking names. There is a Valhalla, New York, and a Valhalla, South Carolina. Many ski lodges and restaurants have Viking names as well.

There have also been many books, movies, and television shows based on the Vikings. Thor, the Viking god of thunder and lightning, is a comic-book

A Viking replica longship sails across the fjord in Greenland at the start of its 1,900 mile journey to North America in 2001. Adventurers tried to recreate Leif Eriksson's voyage to the New World 1,000 years ago.

The Viking mission to Mars took the first close-up pictures of the surface of Mars, and it sampled the soil.

superhero. There is even a football team in Minnesota called the Vikings along with the NASA Viking Mission to Mars.

Spending time with the Vikings was great. But now it is time to leave their world of adventure. We are glad you came with us. Time travel is always more fun with friends. To the time machine!

Farewell Fellow Explorer,

I just wanted to take a moment to tell you a little about the real "Max and me." I am a children's book author and Max is a small, fluffy, white dog. I almost named him Marshmallow because of how he looks. However, he seems to think he's human—so only a more dignified name would do. Max also thinks that he is a large, powerful dog. He fearlessly chases after much larger dogs in the neighborhood. Max was thrilled when the artist for this book drew him as a dog several times his size. He felt that someone in the art world had finally captured his true spirit.

In real life, Max is quite a traveler. I have taken him to nearly every state while doing research for different books. We live in Florida so when we go north I have to pack a sweater for him. When we were in Oregon, it rained and I was glad I brought his raincoat. None of this gear is necessary when time traveling. My "take-off" spot is the computer station and as always Max sits faithfully by my side.

Best Wishes,
Elaine & Max (a small dog with big dreams)

Timeline

793	First recorded Viking raid occurs.
793–1066	Vikings conduct raids throughout Europe.
800	Three major Viking kingdoms develop in Norway, Sweden, and Denmark.
870	Vikings settle in Iceland.
911	Vikings settle in the Normandy region of France.
982	Vikings settle in Greenland.
1000	Leif Eriksson arrives in North America.
1002–1016	Major Viking raids in England.
1100	The Vikings' power lessens.
1962	Researchers find evidence of a Viking settlement in Newfoundland, Canada.

Glossary

barter—To trade one item for another.

boar—A type of wild pig.

brooch—A pin.

captive—A person taken prisoner.

cargo—Goods carried on a vessel.

custom—Something done regularly.

drakkar—A Viking warship.

fjords—Inlets that lead out to the sea.

funeral pyre—A mound of material on which a dead body is burned.

hearth—A fireplace.

prow—The front of a ship.

sod—Grassy soil.

Thing—A Viking assembly where legal questions are decided.

For More Information

Berger, Melvin, and Gilda Berger. *The Real Vikings: Craftsmen, Traders, and Fearsome Raiders*. Washington, D.C.: National Geographic, 2003.

Glaser, Jason. *Leif Eriksson*. Mankato, Minn.: Capstone Press, 2005.

Gravett, Christopher. *Going to War in Viking Times*. New York: Franklin Watts, 2001.

Green, Jen. *Gods and Goddesses in the Daily Lives of the Vikings*. Columbus, Ohio: Peter Bedrick Books, 2003.

Hopkins, Andrea. *Viking Longships*. New York: Powerkids Press, 2002.

Martell, Hazel Mary. *Food & Feasts With the Vikings*. Parsippany, N.J.: New Discovery Books, 1995.

Wright, Rachel, *The Viking News*. Cambridge, Mass.: Candlewick Press, 1998.

Internet Addresses

BBC: The Vikings

<http://www.bbc.co.uk/schools/vikings/index.shtml>

Check out this Web site to learn more about the Vikings. Do not miss the Activities section for some fun Viking games.

Nova Online/The Vikings

<http://www.pbs.org/wgbh/nova/vikings>

Visit this Web site to explore what life was like in a Viking village.

The Smithsonian Institution, National Museum of Natural History, "Vikings: The North Atlantic Saga"

<http://www.mnh.si.edu/vikings/start.html>

Index

A
All-Father, 28
Althing, 16
amber, 25

B
brooch, 20, 39, 40

C
cargo, 23
Christianity, 14, 32
classes, 15
clothing, 39–40
Columbus,
    Christopher, 9

D
drakkers, 23–24

E
Eric the Red, 15
Eriksson, Leif, 9, 15,
    26, 41

F
fjords, 22, 41
food, 30, 36–38
Frey, 29

Freya, 29
funeral pyre, 31

H
"Hall of the Slain," 30
housing, 33–35
Hugin, 28

K
knarrs, 23

L
Loki, 29–30
longhouses, 33–34

M
mead, 37
monastery, 11
monk, 11
Munin, 28

N
nobles, 16–17
Norsemen, 6
Northmen, 6

O
Odin, 28–29, 30
Old Norse, 8, 9

R
raiders 11–14
religion, 14, 28–32
runes, 21

S
ships, 22–24, 31
slavery, 12, 17
Sleipnir, 28
society, 15–18

T
Things, 15–16
Thor, 29, 41
timber, 25
trade, 25–27

V
Valhalla, 30, 41
Viking Age, 14
Vineland, 9–10

W
Well of Wisdom, 28
Woden, 28–29
work, 18, 19–21